ON THE SHORES

OF ETERNITY

Boundless Energy

Perfect Digestion

The Way of the Wizard

Overcoming Addictions

Raid on the Inarticulate

The Path to Love

The Seven Spiritual Laws for Parents

The Love Poems of Rumi
(edited by Deepak Chopra; translated by
Deepak Chopra and Fereydoun Kia)

Healing the Heart

Everyday Immortality

Lords of Light

ON THE SHORES

Poems from Tagore

OF ETERNITY

on Immortality and Beyond

NEW ENGLISH VERSIONS BY
Deepak Chopra

Harmony Books *New York*

Published by Harmony Books, 201 East 50th Street, New York,
New York 10022. Member of the Crown Publishing Group.

Random House, Inc. New York, Toronto, London, Sydney, Auckland
www.randomhouse.com

HARMONY BOOKS is a registered trademark and Harmony Books
colophon is a trademark of Random House, Inc.

Printed in the United States of America

Design by Barbara Sturman

Library of Congress Cataloging-in-Publication Data
Tagore, Rabindranath, 1861–1941.
[Poems. English. Selections]
On the shores of eternity : poems from Tagore on
immortality and beyond / Deepak Chopra.
p.   cm.
1. Tagore, Rabindranath, 1861–1941—Translations into English.
I. Chopra, Deepak.   II. Title.
PK1722.A2C49   1999
891'.4414—dc21   99-20930
                                          CIP

ISBN 0-609-60564-X

10 9 8 7 6 5 4 3 2 1

First Edition

Acknowledgments

❦

Thank you to the staff at The Chopra Center for Well Being, in particular Carolyn Rangel and Jennie Pugh for their boundless energy and enthusiasm on this project.

A Note to the Reader

❧

$\mathcal{I}$ would like to share with the reader the exact process that went into the creation of these poems. I read a number of translations of Tagore's work, including his own original translations from Bengali to English. (In fact, it was W. B. Yeats, the great Irish poet, who helped Tagore with those translations.) I then asked myself how these beautiful sentiments of Tagore could be articulated in the language of the new millennium. The result is what you see. Sometimes I have added a new interpretation, introduced rhyme and meter, or substituted metaphors that are more meaningful to our lives today. At other times I inserted an original phrase or two. I also consulted my Bengali friends so they could reassure me that this modern version of the poems not only reflected the mind of Tagore but also portrayed the worldview of one of our most profound wisdom traditions—the Vedic philosophy that spawned the consciousness and genius of Tagore.

Purists may be offended by my taking these liberties with a literary giant like Tagore. However, my intentions come from a place of innocence and a strong desire to make people aware that Tagore is as relevant today as he was in Edwardian times.

Introduction

A DANCE BEYOND DEATH

❦

The scrawled note came from a stranger, but it had a familiar ring:

"I thought I was getting over my fear of death, until I had to witness my dear grandmother dying last year. The final stages took twelve hours, and when she became aware of her surroundings at the end, all I saw in her eyes was fear and panic. She loved and cared for me so much—I can hardly stand this being so traumatic for her. Please help me, I'm haunted by her eyes."

Dying is a natural process, but our attitudes toward it can be very unnatural. The fear of death witnessed here stems from deep emotions rooted far in the past. Whatever you resist you will fear. When people are dying, they often try to make it go away by saying, "This isn't happening to me, it can't be true. Something will save me." As the process continues, resistance makes it more and more painful.

You can be terribly afraid of dying long before it happens, which is why our destructive emotions need attention now. I can think of no more healing words than those of India's greatest modern writer, the poet Tagore. When I want to know "the most intimate truths of the universe," I turn to him. That phrase is his own, for Tagore knew that the most profound subjects—love, truth, compassion, birth, and death—were his. Many others have written about love and death, but no one has joined them together with the passion of Tagore. He actually saw himself as death's beloved. When he cries, "Death, oh my death, whisper to me! For you alone have I kept watch day after day," you can hear a rare emotion, pure ecstasy, in his voice.

You will not find a morbid word anywhere when Tagore talks about death. He transmutes every tremble of anxiety into words of solace and comfort. Actually, comfort wouldn't be the right word, because Tagore is too triumphant to need it: "Because I love this life," he writes, "I know I shall love death as well." Therefore a book of poems dedicated to death has to be offered in the same spirit Tagore always showed, that of a lover kneeling before the mystery of his Lord.

Reading Tagore is like eavesdropping on a citizen of the cosmos. However, he did come from a definite time and place. Born in Bengal in 1861, Rabindranath Tagore astonished the literary world when he published a little book called *Gītāñjalī* in 1912—it is still his best-known work. Most of the poems gathered here are taken from it. He was the first Asian to win the Nobel Prize for literature, which happened quickly, in 1913. He also painted, lectured, and founded schools and a university. Showered with praise and fame, he became a saint in his homeland and wandered the world to great acclaim until his death in 1941.

These are the bare facts of a great life. Yet the cosmic dimension of Tagore's mind are what capture our attention on these pages. His voice is often humble—he calls himself a "hollow reed carried over hill and dale," and God is the flutist playing endless songs through him. But this humble instrument seems to know God personally. He is intimate with death as well, seeing in him another face of his Lord. To be so deeply religious and yet to give voice to the everyday feelings that we all have are Tagore's unique gifts. For Tagore had no need to romanticize or gloss over any feelings: "Don't be ashamed of tears," he says. "The earth's tears keep her flowers blooming."

The first-time reader of these poems will be fascinated by their emotion and their music. Above all, that is what I have tried to convey in these new translations. Some are very free interpretations (as in "A Note on the Door," which uses the image of a car honking at the curb where Tagore would have been used to a horse and carriage), but I have tried always to maintain the sense of his logic. It is never ordinary logic, for Tagore was also a spiritual teacher whose view of the world turns our everyday perspective upside down. He saw the soul as much more real than any material object, and because of his complete confidence in spiritual reality, he sang of death as a joyful voyage back home.

It's important to realize that Tagore wasn't talking about going to heaven. "Home" meant expanded awareness, the return to God-consciousness that is achieved through enlightenment. In one of his most beautiful sayings, he declares, "Dying is exhaustion, but ending is perfection." In other words, the body dies when it has become too fatigued and worn out to continue, but for our spirits there is no end until we become perfected in consciousness.

I would like to explain why this is not just a religious belief and not merely Eastern. As a physician I have been in the emergency room with hundreds of dying people. For the most part I see them going through definite stages. At some point in the throes of a heart attack or some massive trauma, it dawns on patients that they aren't going to make it. Panic ensues, then for a few moments intense resistance, followed by resignation. I am sure that denial and anger are also going on. The entire range of the dying process, as we are now familiar with it, occurs. If you have someone with a chronic illness like cancer or AIDS, the process can take months, or years. In the ER there is no time for that.

Yet it doesn't occur to us that this whole drama may be rooted in our belief that death is a form of suffering. Tagore doesn't accept such suffering; to him it is the outcome of lack of preparation. In our society the subject of death is still taboo; no one has taught us how to die in advance, what the New Testament calls "dying unto death." In Tagore we find an exuberance in the face of death, a joy in the anticipation of it, precisely because he is so supremely prepared for it. You might wonder how he did this so completely, but Tagore gives us the answer himself: He went to the core of inner silence.

What did this silence tell him? First it made him aware that death is always stalking us, every moment of our lives, not as an enemy but as part of the Unknown that surrounds existence. You have only to look over your shoulder to see that death is a little closer than the last time you looked. Having faced this fact, should you live in perpetual anxiety? For Tagore this knowledge made life magical, because he was forced to change his priorities. "Things that I longed for and things that I pursued, let them pass away," Tagore writes. "Instead let me truly possess what I overlooked and ignored." What would these overlooked things be? Harmony, laughter, compassion—and above all, love.

Silence also allowed him to gain a detachment that had pure joy in it. To understand this you have to appreciate that Tagore's mind isn't the mind of an individual but the mind of an entire spiritual culture. He is the point of a sword held in the hand of many centuries. This tradition holds that you are not your body or your intellect or your ego. These are part of the scenery, but you are the seer. The world of forms, which includes my body and personality, is subject to change. But all change has to occur against the background of nonchange. When I am in touch with my core, I realize clearly that death happens only to the changing body and not to me.

Reading Tagore, you see that this is not just an intellectual understanding but a true experience. His expression emerges with great personal conviction. Thus he can say, "I shall enter the same unknown that was ever known to me." Birth and death are twins, the opposite sides of the unknown, one door leading in, the other out. He uses a beautiful, humble image here: Dying feels terrifying because we are like babies pulled from our mother's breast who cry out, only to be consoled in the next instant when her other breast appears.

If we all had access to Tagore's perspective, would it not alleviate the suffering of millions of people? I have seen religious people express peace in the face of death, but I would suggest that often this is emotionally based on or supported by mere belief. I have mixed feelings about this, because we need to know from real experience, not just a leap of faith, what death is about. We find this not by attacking the problem of death directly but indirectly. The question "Who am I?" contains the answers to all the bigger questions about the soul, God, and the afterlife. Tagore knows himself with incredible clarity and confidence. He knows that his true home is eternity. He isn't going anywhere after he dies, because eternity has no past, present, or future.

Science has come along to verify this very notion. Material things are solid to the touch, but at the quantum level, every atom is 99.999 percent empty space, and solidity dissolves into a bundle of vibrating energy. This energy was never created and can never be destroyed. It flickers in and out of the prequantum region millions of times per second. In a very real sense, this is the only birth and the only death we will ever experience. Far from being a unique event, our bodies die a hundred times before your eye can read a single word of this sentence. What we call death is a misnomer; it is just the cessation of the process of appearing and disappearing. With our last breath we go back to where there is no time. What we call dying is the giving up of birth and death together.

At this moment your body could not be alive without death. Billions of cells have to perish to bring new ones to life. You could not think or feel or dream if your mind did not allow your old thoughts to die away and make room for the new.

So it is a myth to think that death is out there waiting for us. Death is here with us, tied into the flow of life. There is a wonderful saying, "You will never be more alive than you are at this moment, and you will never be more dead than you are this moment." Your goal, then, should be to experience yourself as fully now as you can, and in doing that you will make peace with any fear, any doubt, any resistance. Don't see yourself as struggling to remain alive against all obstacles; see yourself as a river that accepts all change because change is natural as you move from one life stage to the next. How amazing that Tagore knew this and could express it in a beautiful aphorism: "The stars are not afraid to flicker out like fireflies."

Unlike Tagore most people do not embrace the region beyond material existence. It is sealed off from us by a wall built by the five senses, which make us trust things we can touch and see, and distrust what we cannot. We can't scale this wall or smash through it, so we imagine all sorts of horrors on the other side. Tagore saw through the wall, as if it were transparent. What he saw looming on the other side wasn't heaven or hell or even a personified God. He saw a paradox. He saw the unknown that he always knew.

To me, this could mean only one thing: We are already as involved with death as we will ever be. We are surrounded by eternity; the horizon is infinite in all directions. At the most primordial level of existence we participate in a timeless reality. Why wait for a crisis, the moment of dying, to explore the infinite and eternal? They are available every day. This is the level of time to which Tagore never forgot to pay attention. He doesn't "solve" the mystery of death; he lays it before us in all its paradox. He speaks of the timeless with an awe that befits anyone who must, after all, live in time.

Tagore also teaches us that perspective is all. Whether we can solve death's mystery or not, certainly we can start living in it. We can become kinder and more considerate by seeing ourselves all sharing the aspect of eternity. (I don't think anyone could read the last poem of this book, "I Will Come to You," without deep emotion and an inner promise to be more compassionate.) We can touch the fringes of the unknown by our own delving into love.

Because Tagore links it to birth, there is a child-like tone to dying in these poems, but also a wisdom that makes death different from birth. Many books have offered solace to those who are facing death, but here is an opening to wise innocence. His words are so essential we have all used them since we were five or six years old, yet what magic emerges when Tagore combines them, as in this little verse I've entitled "A Kiss":

The night kissed the fading day
With a whisper.
"I am death, your mother,
From me you will get new birth."

The reader will find many poems like this, and it is rare for any of the poems not to touch on innocence at some time. To realize that death is an illusion, you either have to be very sophisticated or very simple. Tagore was both. I have included two dozen of his sayings, mere jottings he gathered together as *Stray Birds*. Although it is easy to be astonished by anything Tagore wrote, these aphorisms are pure crystals of wise innocence:

Renunciation
I live in the world afraid to lose anything
Take me to your world where I can lose
    everything.

Kiss
God shows His love by kissing the finite
Man shows his by kissing the infinite.

Silence
Words cling to the dead like dust
Silence washes their souls.

I am awed by these stray birds—every word is personal, every word is universal. Those who met Tagore in his eighty years described him as one of the great souls of our age; Einstein considered him a sage. From what we learn in these poems, he certainly lived his own words. He kissed the infinite; he was not afraid to lose everything. And in this book, he allows us to approach death not with dusty words but with a silence that washes the soul.

ON THE SHORES

OF ETERNITY

Whisper to Me!

O thou the fulfillment of my life
Death, my death
Whisper to me!

For you alone have I kept watch day after day
And borne the pangs and joys of life.
For you alone have I saved all that I have,
    that I am,
That I hope.
Flowing to you in secret.

Like an eager bride I weave
The garland for your neck and the flowers for
    my hair.
It will be our wedding day, O death,
And when the last guest is gone,
I will steal away from my empty house
To lie with thou in the solitude of night.

The Storm

Boatman, are you lost on the sea tonight?
The wild sea whose winds rip your sails
The sky falling on you like a beast with fangs
And the darkness poisonous with fear.
Waves are crashing on an unseen shore,
But the boatman must cross tonight.

His journey is secret
No one knows the name of the lover he meets
As his sails startle the night with whiteness.
But somewhere a lamp is burning
In a silent courtyard,
And she waits.

What passionate quest makes you fearless
Of the night and the storm?
Are you taking her a horde of rubies and pearls?
Ah no, the boatman has no such treasure to offer,

Only a song on his lips and a white rose in
    his hand
And she smiles, waiting for a glimpse of him
Sitting beside her lamp
On the other side.

Through the howling wind she hears him call
    her name
She whose name no one knows,
When will he come? Hours still
Or is it years?
He will land without a sound,
No one will see him run to her
But light will fill that house and bless its very dust
When the boatman has landed
On the shores of Eternity.

What Will You Give?

What will you give
When death knocks at your door?

The fullness of my life—
The sweet wine of autumn days and summer
    nights,
My little hoard gleaned through the years,
And hours rich with living.

These will be my gift.
When death knocks at my door.

A Note on the Door

I'm not home anymore
I left you my keys
And the deed to the house—
It's yours

Just say a few kind words when you can
You were good to me all these years
And I got a lot more than I gave

Take care of yourself, you whom I loved
I hear a horn honking at the curb
And one more light is left to put out.

The Stars Look On

The day will come
When the sight of this earth will be lost
I will take my leave in silence
As the stars look on

I know the sun will rise again
The hours will still bring pleasure and pain
In heaving waves.

When I think of the end, time crumbles
I see by the light of death
That the lowliest existence is rare
And the worst moments are precious

What I longed for will be set aside

The things I pursued in vain—

Let them pass

Let me turn

To things I overlooked

And carelessly threw away

To possess them truly until they are mine

As the stars look on.

In Life or Death

Here I am, spilling over with you
Like a cup overflowing with wine!

You see through my eyes
You hear through my ears
You weave words in my mind
And your joy sets them to music.

O give yourself to me in love
Then feel it pouring back to you again!

You are my poet, Lord!
And I am your poem.

Power

God moves swiftly
The leaves are born and die
God moves slowly
The stars are born and die.

Nothing to Wear

It was just turning dawn when my journey began
And the road looked beautiful under the sky.
Don't ask me what I'm taking, I have nothing
    to wear
My bags are empty, and my hands are bare.

A light will be shining when I arrive
The evening star where music is heard.
On second thought, I'll be wearing my ring
What more need I take to marry the king?

The Answer

I heard the sea and asked,

"What language is that?"

The sea replied,

"The language of eternal questions."

I saw the sky and asked,

"What holds the answer?"

The sky replied,

"The language of eternal silence."

Understanding

When I think of ages past
That have floated down the stream
Of life and love and death,
I feel how free it makes us
To pass away.

Beauty

Let life be as beautiful as summer flowers
And death as beautiful as autumn leaves.

First Light

When I was born and saw the light
I was no stranger in this world
Something inscrutable, shapeless, and
    without words
Appeared in the form of my mother.

So when I die, the same unknown will
    appear again
As ever known to me,
And because I love this life
I will love death as well.

My Parting Words

On the day I left home
I had some parting words:

"Unsurpassable were the things I've seen,
Sweet the honey in the flower that expanded
    on an ocean of light,
Infinite was the playhouse where I performed
    my play,
Before I caught sight of the invisible One.
My whole body thrilled with a touch from Him
    who has no touch
And even now every limb is quivering as I depart."

So on the day when time crumbles for you
Remember this parting word.

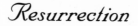

Resurrection

If you weep because the sun has gone out
Your tears may blind you to the stars.

Awe

When we played together I never asked who
   you were.
You called me from sleep under my window
And you led the chase from meadow to woods.
My life was so boisterous that I was never afraid
   of you
You were just my friend— I echoed your songs
And never asked what they meant.

Now playtime is over
And I've suddenly gone blind.
What is this?
Why has the world taken off its sandals
And dropped to its knees
As I bow my head under the silent stars?

A Stone Will Melt

I know what it will be like—
My pride will go to the wall
My life will burst its bonds in exceeding pain
And my empty heart will sob out in music like a
    hollow reed.

The stone will melt in tears
Because I can't remain closed to you forever.
I can't escape without being conquered.

From the blue sky an eye will gaze down
To summon me in silence.
I will receive death utterly at your feet.

I know what it will be like.

Change

I sit at my window gazing
The world passes by, nods to me
And is gone.

Acceptance

This time I won't struggle.
When the moment comes,
I will let Him take the helm
In an instant the thing will be done
It was vain to fight it.

So take away your hands
And put up with this defeat, my heart.
Sit perfectly still where He tells you to
And count it good fortune.
Stop running around so desperately
To protect your little lamp from the wind.
Can't you remember after all this time?
We have to be wise and wait in the dark
Spreading out cushions on the floor
So that whenever He pleases
My Lord will sit with us.

The Silent Harp

I can't wait to die and be deathless.
No more sailing from harbor to harbor
In my storm-wrecked boat.
No more diving for pearls where none can
    be found.

I seek a deeper abyss
A soundless place
Where I can take the harp of my life
And tune it to the notes of forever.

Then, when it has sobbed out its last refrain
I will take my silent harp
And lay it at the feet of silence.

Troubadour

My songs did it all.
They made me seek you from door to door
And with them I felt my way
Searching and touching this world.

They taught me all the lessons I ever learned
They showed me secret paths
And faint stars on the horizon of my heart.

Every day they took me into the mysteries of
    pleasure and pain
Until they got me here
In the evening of my journey
To the gates of the unknown palace.

Unmanifest

What you are you do not see.
What you see—that you are not.

Salutation

I bow to you, my God, just one bow
And suddenly my senses expand
Touching every corner
Of the world at your feet.

My head falls low
Like a rain cloud in July about to burst
My songs gather into one rushing stream
That flows into a sea of silence.
My whole life makes its way back like
    homesick cranes
Flying night and day to reach their
    mountain nests.

In one bow to Thee.

Living the Infinite

It pleased you to make me endless

You empty this frail vessel over and over
Then fill it with fresh life again.
You carry me like a hollow reed over hill and dale
Eternally breathing new melodies through me.
At the immortal touch of your hand
My little heart loses itself in joy.

Still you pour into me, and still there is room
    to fill.

Surprise

Life is just the perpetual surprise that I exist.

Illusion

Why do I die again and again?
To prove that life is inexhaustible.

Incarnation

I thought the journey was over
When my powers came to an end.
The path before me was closed,
The provisions were exhausted
And the time had come to take shelter
In some small dark corner.

But your will knows no end in me.
When the old song dies on the tongue,
A new one springs forth from the heart
And where the old tracks have been swept away
A new country is revealed in all its wonder.

Immortality

The stars are not afraid to flicker out like fireflies.
And you?

Giving

Life is given to us
Then we earn it by giving it back.

Longing

When a flower opens, do you know what it wishes?
"Please, world, do not fade."

Can't You Hear Him?

Have you not heard his silent steps?
At every moment and every age
Every day and every night
In the fragrant springtime and down the frozen path
In the rainy gloom of a summer storm
When his thunderous chariot passes overhead
In sorrow after sorrow, joy after joy
That press upon my heart—

He comes, he comes, he ever comes.

Priceless

The coin of life is stamped with death
So that what we buy will be truly precious.

Prepare, Prepare

It was getting dark. The day's work was done,
and we were sure the last guest had arrived, so
we closed the doors and locked them. Only
someone happened to say, "Isn't the king coming?"
We laughed and said, "What king? You must
be joking."

When a tap came at the door we ignored it. The
lights were already out and we went to bed. Only
a small voice said, "That was the messenger." We
yawned in his face. "No, it was just the wind."

It was after midnight when a sound arose like
distant thunder. The shaking earth and trembling
walls troubled us in our sleep. Someone said it
was the sound of wheels. We murmured drowsily,
"Go back to sleep, it's just a cloudburst."

There was still no light when the drums began to bang. The voice came, "Wake up, you don't have time to waste!" We sat up, hearts quaking, and thought we'd die with fear. Someone ran back from the window. "My God, I see a flag!" We jumped to our feet shouting, "Prepare, prepare, there's no time for delay."

The king has come, but where are the lights, where are the flowers? Where is the throne to seat him on? Shame, shame! No banquet hall, no decorations? Someone said, "It's pointless, what's the use? Just meet him at the door with empty hands. Walk him alone through the bare rooms."

So that's what we did. We threw open the doors
and gave a blast on the bugle. In the dead of
night he came to our dreary house. Thunder
roared in the sky, and the air shuddered with
lightning. We spread a tattered rug on the floor.
It was all we could do when death appeared,
our king of the fearful night.

Mystery

Where is the unseen flame
Whose sparks are the stars?

Perfection

To die is exhausting
To end is perfection.

Knowing

Who do you long for?
The one I can feel in the night
But cannot see in the day.

Invisible

Put out the light when you wish
I will know your darkness and love it.

Consumed

When I die my body will be turned to ashes.
My hands and arms
Will dance in your whirling wind
And my life will rise up in a burning heat
To mingle with the purity of your flame!

Victory!

In a burst of light
The heart of night is pierced.
Your flashing sword cuts through all doubts
You, the light, so white and terrible
Come to me in a march of fire
Brandishing your torch on high—
Victory!
And death dies in a burst of splendor.

Kiss

God shows His love by kissing the finite
Man shows his by kissing the infinite.

Formless

I bragged that I knew you
I started passing your picture around.
But when they asked, "Who is that?"
I couldn't reply,
Only saying, "I don't know."
So they laughed and went away in scorn.

You just sat there smiling.

I put you in every word
The secrets poured out from my heart.
But when they read the words
They asked, "What are you talking about?"
I couldn't reply,
Only saying, "I don't know."
So they laughed again and went away in scorn.

And you?
You just sat there smiling.

Soul

One day we will learn that death cannot steal
Anything gained by the soul.

A Dance Beyond Death

The same stream of life that runs through my veins
Runs through the world and dances in rhythmic
measure.
It is the same life that shoots in joy through the
dust of the earth
In numberless blades of grass,
Breaking in waves of leaves and flowers.
The same life that rocks the cradle of birth
and death
In the ocean of eternal existence.
My life is made glorious by touching this world
And my pride is from knowing
That the life-throb of ages dances in my blood
at this moment.

Blossom

Tears are no shame.
It is the tears of the earth that keep her flowers
  blooming.

Silence

Words cling to the dead like dust
Silence washes their souls.

Change and the Changeless

The fireflies went to school
And said to the stars,
"We learned that you are going to burn out
    one day."
The stars made no reply.

Gratitude

The day is thanked for the flowers
That blossomed in the night.

Renunciation

I live in the world afraid to lose anything
Take me to your world where I can lose
    everything.

Beyond Birth and Death

Oh, to be free!

Where the mind is without fear and the head is
    held high
Where knowledge has no boundaries
Where the world has not been walled off into
    fragments
Where words come out from the depths of truth
Where the work is tireless and reaches for
    perfection
Where the clear stream of reason is not parched
In a desert of old habits
Where thoughts can expand without end.

Into this heaven of freedom, my soul, let us go!

Out of Time

Hurry up!
We're almost out of time
Days and nights fly by
Ages bloom and fade like flowers
We have to scramble for our chances
We're too poor to be late—

And so I rushed to save every minute
While squandering away hours
To anyone who wanted them.

And when the frantic race was over
I could see the finish line
Bursting with fear lest I be too late
Only to find at the last minute

That yet there is time.

At the Edge

What a beautiful bracelet you wear
Decked out with stars and entwined with gems
But to me your sword is more beautiful
With its curve of lightning
Like the outspread wings of some divine bird
Perfectly poised in the angry red light of sunset.

It quivers like one last tremble of life in an ecstasy
    of pain
It shines like the pure flame that turns the senses
    to ashes
In one fierce flash.

Beautiful is your bracelet, Lord, bedecked with
    stars and gems
But who could imagine the working of your sword?
Terrible to behold or even to think of
At the stroke of death.

The Messenger

Death, your servant is at my door
He came across the unknown sea
To say that you are calling me.

The night is dark and my heart is afraid
I must turn on the light
And make him feel welcome.
Tears will flow as I bow to him
Placing at his feet the treasure of my life.

He will go back with his errand done,
Leaving a dark shadow behind.
And my little self will be waiting in this
    empty house
As an offering to you.

Nostalgia

I was homesick today
For one sweet hour across the sea of time.

Grieving

When you died, you left behind
The sadness of the Eternal.
You painted the horizon with sunset colors
A track of tears swept from the earth to
    love's heaven.

Clasped in your dear arms,
Life and death joined in me
Like a wedding vow.

I can see you standing on the balcony
Where the end and the beginning of all
    things meet.
You want to take me through that door
Holding the cup of death to my lips
As you fill it with life from your own.

A Kiss

The night kissed the fading day
With a whisper.
"I am death, your mother,
From me you will get new birth."

"I Will Come to You"

On a sultry August night when the murky sky
    hid the stars
A young man slept outside the walls of the city
Upagupta, the disciple of Buddha.
He stirs as a foot lightly touches his chest
To the tinkling sound of silver anklets.
"Who is it?"
His vision clears, and he sees a dancing girl
Starred with jewels, drunk on the wine of
    her youth.

She lowers her lamp to stare at his face
Made beautiful by austerity.
"Forgive me, young holy man,
But the dusty earth isn't a fit place for your bed,
Come to my house and be my guest tonight."
The monk replies, "Go your way, woman,
    when the time is right,

I will come to you."
Suddenly the night shows its teeth in a snarl
    of lightning
A storm prowls the sky
And the girl trembles.

Spring—
The air is filled with music from a distant flute
Fragrant blossoms weigh down the trees
Leaving the town empty—everyone has gone to
    the woods for the festival.
One lone monk walks the streets listening to
    love-sick birds sleepless overhead in the
    mango trees.
Upagupta walks outside the gates and stands
    beneath the ramparts.

What woman is this dying at his feet, her body
    blackened with sores
Driven away from the sight of the town?

The young man sits by her side, taking her head
    on his knees
He moistens her lips with water and rubs oil on
    her sores.
"Who are you, merciful one?" she asks.
Upagupta replies,
"I told you I would come to you when the time
    is right
And now I am here."

Index of Poems

❧

About the Author

❧

DEEPAK CHOPRA has written twenty-three books, which have been translated into thirty-five languages. He is also the author of more than thirty audio and videotape series, including five critically acclaimed programs on public television. Chopra currently serves as the director for educational programs at The Chopra Center for Well Being in La Jolla, California.